SPORTACULAR AFGHANS

Get your game on with afghans for good sports! Aficionados are sure to appreciate the realistic details of the appliqués.

18

BOWLING ALLEY - 2

GOLF GREEN - 10

POKER TABLE - 18

POOL TABLE - 24

SLOT MACHINE - 32

GENERAL INSTRUCTIONS - 41

YARN INFORMATION - 47

MEET THE DESIGNER: KAREN BARNES - 48

24

LEISURE ARTS, INC. • Maumelle, Arkansas

BOWLING ALLEY

AFGHAN NO. 1

BOWLING ALLEY

EASY +

Finished Size: 44½″ x 62″ (113 cm x 157.5 cm)

SHOPPING LIST

Yarn

MEDIUM 4

(Medium Weight)

[3.5 ounces, 170 yards (100 grams, 156 meters) per skein**]**:

- ☐ Black - 9 skeins
- ☐ White - 3 skeins
- ☐ Red - 1 skein

[5 ounces, 251 yards (142 grams, 230 meters) per skein**]**:

- ☐ Gold - 6 skeins
- ☐ Blue - 1 skein

Crochet Hook

- ☐ Size I (5.5 mm) **or** size needed for gauge

Additional Supplies

- ☐ Pins (for Finishing)
- ☐ Yarn needle

GAUGE INFORMATION

In pattern, 2 repeats (12 sts) = 3″ (7.5 cm);
10 rows = 4¾″ (12 cm)
Each Strip = 3¼″ (8.25 cm)

Gauge Swatch:
3¼″w x 4¾″h (8.25 cm x 12 cm)
Work same as Plain Strip for 10 rows: 13 sts.

STITCH GUIDE

HALF DOUBLE CROCHET 2 TOGETHER (abbreviated hdc2tog) (uses next 2 hdc)
★ YO, insert hook in **next** hdc, YO and pull up a loop; repeat from ★ once **more**, YO and draw through all 5 loops on hook **(counts as one hdc)**.

ALLEY

Plain Strip (Make 2)

With Gold, ch 14.

Row 1: Sc in second ch from hook, ★ skip next 2 chs, 5 dc in next ch, skip next 2 chs, sc in next ch; repeat from ★ once **more**: 13 sts.

Row 2 (Right side): Ch 3 **(counts as first dc, now and throughout)**, turn; 2 dc in first sc, skip next 2 dc, sc in next dc, skip next 2 dc, 5 dc in next sc, skip next 2 dc, sc in next dc, skip next 2 dc, 3 dc in last sc.

Note: Loop a short piece of yarn around any stitch to mark Row 2 as **right** side **and** bottom edge.

Row 3: Ch 1, turn; sc in first dc, ★ skip next 2 dc, 5 dc in next sc, skip next 2 dc, sc in next dc; repeat from ★ once **more**.

Row 4: Ch 3, turn; 2 dc in first sc, skip next 2 dc, sc in next dc, skip next 2 dc, 5 dc in next sc, skip next 2 dc, sc in next dc, skip next 2 dc, 3 dc in last sc.

Repeat Rows 3 and 4 for pattern until Strip measures approximately 41″ (104 cm) from beginning ch, ending by working a **right** side row.

Last Row: Ch 1, turn; sc in first 2 dc, hdc in next 3 sts, sc in next 3 dc, hdc in next 3 sts, sc in last 2 dc.

Trim: Ch 1, do **not** turn; work 164 sc evenly spaced across end of rows; working in free loops of beginning ch **(Fig. 3b, page 43)**, sc in ch at base of first sc and in each ch across; work 164 sc evenly spaced across end of rows; slip st in first sc on Last Row, finish off: 354 sc (13 sts across each short edge and 164 sc across each long edge).

1st & 7th Arrow Strips

Work same as Plain Strip for 3 rows: 13 sts.

Row 4: Ch 3, turn; 2 dc in first sc, skip next 2 dc, sc in next dc changing to Black **(Fig. 4a, page 44)**, cut Gold; skip next 2 dc, 5 dc in next sc changing to Gold in last dc made **(Fig. 4b, page 44)**, cut Black; skip next 2 dc, sc in next dc, skip next 2 dc, 3 dc in last sc.

Complete same as Plain Strip.

2nd & 6th Arrow Strips

Work same as Plain Strip for 7 rows: 13 sts.

Row 8: Ch 3, turn; 2 dc in first sc, skip next 2 dc, sc in next dc changing to Black, cut Gold; skip next 2 dc, 5 dc in next sc changing to Gold in last dc made, cut Black; skip next 2 dc, sc in next dc, skip next 2 dc, 3 dc in last sc.

Complete same as Plain Strip.

3rd & 5th Arrow Strips

Work same as Plain Strip for 11 rows: 13 sts.

Row 12: Ch 3, turn; 2 dc in first sc, skip next 2 dc, sc in next dc changing to Black, cut Gold; skip next 2 dc, 5 dc in next sc changing to Gold in last dc made, cut Black; skip next 2 dc, sc in next dc, skip next 2 dc, 3 dc in last sc.

Complete same as Plain Strip.

4th Arrow Strip

Work same as Plain Strip for 15 rows: 13 sts.

Row 16: Ch 3, turn; 2 dc in first sc, skip next 2 dc, sc in next dc changing to Black, cut Gold; skip next 2 dc, 5 dc in next sc changing to Gold in last dc made, cut Black; skip next 2 dc, sc in next dc, skip next 2 dc, 3 dc in last sc.

Complete same as Plain Strip.

Assembly

Strips are joined in the following order:
Plain, 1st Arrow, 2nd Arrow, 3rd Arrow, 4th Arrow, 5th Arrow, 6th Arrow, 7th Arrow, Plain.

Join Strips as follows:
With **wrong** sides and bottoms of 2 Strips together, beginning at top and working through **inside** loops of Trim across long edge, join Gold with sc in first sc on Trim **(see Joining With Sc, page 42)**; sc in each sc across long edge ending in last sc; finish off.

Join remaining Strips in same manner.

Strip Edging

To work joining decrease, YO, insert hook in same sc as strip joining on same Strip, YO and pull up a loop (3 loops on hook), YO, skip Strip joining and insert hook in same sc as strip joining on next Strip, YO and pull up a loop, YO and draw through all 5 loops on hook.

With **right** side of long edge facing and beginning at bottom, join Gold with sc in first sc of Trim; 2 sc in same st, sc in next 162 sc, 3 sc in next sc; working sc across top of Strips and joining decreases at Strip joinings, work 123 sts evenly spaced across to next corner; 3 sc in first sc of Trim, sc in next 162 sc, 3 sc in next sc; working sc across bottom of Strips and joining decreases at Strip joinings, work 123 sts evenly spaced across; join with slip st to first sc, finish off: 582 sts.

Gutter (Make 2)

With Black, ch 26.

Row 1: Sc in second ch from hook, ★ skip next 2 chs, 5 dc in next ch, skip next 2 chs, sc in next ch; repeat from ★ across: 25 sts.

Row 2 (Right side)**:** Ch 3, turn; 2 dc in first sc, skip next 2 dc, sc in next dc, ★ skip next 2 dc, 5 dc in next sc, skip next 2 dc, sc in next dc; repeat from ★ across to last 3 sts, skip next 2 dc, 3 dc in last sc.

Note: Mark Row 2 as **right** side **and** bottom edge.

Row 3: Ch 1, turn; sc in first dc, ★ skip next 2 dc, 5 dc in next sc, skip next 2 dc, sc in next dc; repeat from ★ across.

Row 4: Ch 3, turn; 2 dc in first sc, skip next 2 dc, sc in next dc, ★ skip next 2 dc, 5 dc in next sc, skip next 2 dc, sc in next dc; repeat from ★ across to last 3 sts, skip next 2 dc, 3 dc in last sc.

Repeat Rows 3 and 4 for pattern until Gutter measures approximately 41¾" (106 cm) from beginning ch, ending by working a **right** side row.

Last Row: Ch 1, turn; sc in first 2 dc, hdc in next 3 sts, (sc in next 3 dc, hdc in next 3 sts) 3 times, sc in last 2 dc.

Finish off.

Lay assembled Strips on a flat surface with **right** side facing. Place long edge of Gutter parallel to long edge of Strips, having **right** side facing and bottom edge at the same end. With Black and working from center st of one corner to center st of next corner on Strip Edging and in end of rows across long edge of Gutter, whipstitch pieces together **(Figs. 6a & b, page 45)**.

Repeat on opposite side of Strips with remaining Gutter.

Pit

Row 1: With **right** side of top edge facing, join Black with dc in first sc **(see Joining With Dc, page 42)**; 2 dc in same st, skip next 2 sts, sc in next st, ★ skip next 2 sts, 5 dc in next st, skip next 2 sts, sc in next st; repeat from ★ across to last 3 sts, skip next 2 sts, 3 dc in last sc: 175 sts.

Row 2: Ch 1, turn; sc in first dc, ★ skip next 2 dc, 5 dc in next sc, skip next 2 dc, sc in next dc; repeat from ★ across.

Row 3: Ch 3, turn; 2 dc in first sc, skip next 2 dc, sc in next dc, ★ skip next 2 dc, 5 dc in next sc, skip next 2 dc, sc in next dc; repeat from ★ across to last 3 sts, skip next 2 dc, 3 dc in last sc.

Repeat Rows 2 and 3 for pattern until Pit measures approximately 20″ (51 cm) from Strips, ending by working a **right** side row.

Last Row: Ch 1, turn; sc in first 2 dc, hdc in next 3 sts, (sc in next 3 dc, hdc in next 3 sts) across to last 2 dc, sc in last 2 dc; finish off.

GAME PIECES

Bowling Ball

Rnd 1 (Right side)**:** With Blue, ch 2, 8 sc in second ch from hook; do **not** join, place marker to indicate the beginning of the rnd **(see Markers, page 42)**.

Note: Mark Rnd 1 as **right** side.

Rnd 2: 2 Sc in each sc around: 16 sc.

Rnd 3: (Sc in next sc, 2 sc in next sc) around: 24 sc.

Rnd 4: (Sc in next 2 sc, 2 sc in next sc) around: 32 sc.

Rnd 5: (Sc in next 3 sc, 2 sc in next sc) around: 40 sc.

Rnd 6: (Sc in next 4 sc, 2 sc in next sc) around: 48 sc.

Rnd 7: Sc in each sc around.

Rnd 8: (Sc in next 5 sc, 2 sc in next sc) around: 56 sc.

Rnd 9: Sc in each sc around.

Rnd 10: (Sc in next 6 sc, 2 sc in next sc) around: 64 sc.

Rnd 11: Sc in each sc around.

Rnd 12: (Sc in next 7 sc, 2 sc in next sc) around: 72 sc.

Rnd 13: Sc in each sc around.

Rnd 14: (Sc in next 8 sc, 2 sc in next sc) around: 80 sc.

Rnd 15: Sc in each sc around; slip st in next sc, finish off leaving a long end for sewing.

Bowling Pin (Make 10)

With White, ch 8.

Row 1 (Right side)**:** Sc in second ch from hook and in each ch across: 7 sc.

Note: Mark Row 1 as **right** side.

Row 2: Ch 2 **(does not count as a st, now and throughout)**, turn; 2 hdc in first sc, hdc in next 5 sc, 2 hdc in last sc: 9 hdc.

Row 3: Ch 2, turn; hdc in first hdc and in each hdc across.

Row 4 (Increase row)**:** Ch 2, turn; 2 hdc in first hdc, hdc in next hdc and in each hdc across to last hdc, 2 hdc in last hdc: 11 hdc.

Rows 5-9: Repeat Rows 3 and 4 twice, then repeat Row 3 once **more**: 15 hdc.

Rows 10 and 11: Ch 2, turn; 2 hdc in first hdc, hdc in next hdc and in each hdc across to last hdc, 2 hdc in last hdc: 19 hdc.

Rows 12-16: Ch 2, turn; hdc in first hdc and in each hdc across.

Rows 17-22: Ch 2, turn; beginning in first hdc, hdc2tog, hdc in next hdc and in each hdc across to last 2 hdc, hdc2tog: 7 hdc.

Finish off.

Row 23: With **right** side facing, join Red with slip st in first hdc; ch 2, hdc in first hdc and in each hdc across.

Row 24: Ch 2, turn; hdc in first hdc and in each hdc across; finish off.

Row 25 (Increase row)**:** With **right** side facing, join White with slip st in first hdc; ch 2, 2 hdc in first hdc, hdc in next hdc and in each hdc across to last hdc, 2 hdc in last hdc: 9 hdc.

Row 26: Ch 2, turn; hdc in first hdc and in each hdc across; finish off.

Rows 27 and 28: With Red, repeat Rows 25 and 26: 11 hdc.

Row 29: Repeat Row 25: 13 hdc.

Rows 30-32: Repeat Rows 3 and 4 once, then repeat Row 3 once **more**: 15 hdc.

Row 33: Ch 2, turn; beginning in first hdc, hdc2tog 7 times, hdc in last hdc: 8 hdc.

Row 34: Ch 2, turn; beginning in first hdc, hdc2tog 4 times; finish off leaving a long end for sewing.

FINISHING

Using photo, page 2, as a guide for placement, pin pieces to **right** side of Pit. Sew in place using matching yarn and long ends.

GOLF GREEN

AFGHAN NO. 2

GOLF GREEN

EASY +

Finished Size: 42″ x 64″ (106.5 cm x 162.5 cm)

SHOPPING LIST

Yarn

FOR GOLF COURSE

MEDIUM 4 (Medium Weight)
[3.5 ounces, 170 yards
(100 grams, 156 meters) per skein]:

- ☐ Green - 7 skeins
- ☐ Dk Green - 6 skeins
- ☐ Olive Green - 5 skeins
- ☐ White - 5 yards (4.5 meters)
- ☐ Off White - 150 yards (137 meters)

FOR GAME PIECES

LIGHT 3 (Light Weight)

- ☐ White - 8 yards (7.5 meters)
- ☐ Yellow - 7 yards (6.5 meters)
- ☐ Grey - 5 yards (4.5 meters)
- ☐ Blue - small amount

Crochet Hooks

FOR GOLF COURSE

- ☐ Size I (5.5 mm) **or** size needed for gauge

FOR GAME PIECES

- ☐ Size G (4 mm)

Additional Supplies

- ☐ Pins (for Finishing)
- ☐ Yarn needle
- ☐ Tapestry needle

GAUGE INFORMATION

With larger size hook, in Putting Green pattern,
Rnds 1-5 = 6″ (15.25 cm) diameter

With larger size hook, in Fairway pattern,
14 sts and 14 rows = 4″ (10 cm)

Gauge Swatch: 6″ (15.25 cm) diameter

Work same as Putting Green for 5 rnds: 65 dc.

STITCH GUIDE

TREBLE CROCHET (abbreviated tr)

YO twice, insert hook in st indicated, YO and pull up a loop (4 loops on hook), (YO and draw through 2 loops on hook) 3 times.

SINGLE CROCHET 2 TOGETHER (abbreviated sc2tog)

Pull up a loop in each of next 2 sts, YO and draw through all 3 loops on hook **(counts as one sc)**.

DOUBLE CROCHET 2 TOGETHER (abbreviated dc2tog) (uses next 2 sts)

★ YO, insert hook in **next** st, YO and pull up a loop, YO and draw through 2 loops on hook; repeat from ★ once **more**, YO and draw through all 3 loops on hook **(counts as one dc)**.

GOLF COURSE

Putting Green

Rnd 1 (Right side)**:** With larger size hook and Medium Weight White, ch 3, 13 dc in third ch from hook; skip beginning ch and join with slip st to first dc: 13 dc.

Note: Loop a short piece of yarn around any stitch to mark Rnd 1 as **right** side.

Rnd 2: Ch 2 **(does not count as a st, now and throughout)**, 2 dc in same st as joining and in each dc around; join with slip st to first dc, finish off: 26 dc.

Rnd 3: With **right** side facing and using larger size hook, join Olive Green with slip st in same st as joining; ch 2, 2 dc in same st, dc in next dc, (2 dc in next dc, dc in next dc) around; join with slip st to first dc: 39 dc.

Rnd 4: Ch 2, 2 dc in same st as joining, dc in next 2 dc, (2 dc in next dc, dc in next 2 dc) around; join with slip st to first dc: 52 dc.

Rnd 5: Ch 2, 2 dc in same st as joining, dc in next 3 dc, (2 dc in next dc, dc in next 3 dc) around; join with slip st to first dc: 65 dc.

Rnd 6: Ch 2, 2 dc in same st as joining, dc in next 4 dc, (2 dc in next dc, dc in next 4 dc) around; join with slip st to first dc: 78 dc.

Rnd 7: Ch 2, 2 dc in same st as joining, dc in next 5 dc, (2 dc in next dc, dc in next 5 dc) around; join with slip st to first dc: 91 dc.

Rnd 8: Ch 2, 2 dc in same st as joining, dc in next 6 dc, (2 dc in next dc, dc in next 6 dc) around; join with slip st to first dc: 104 dc.

Rnd 9: Ch 2, 2 dc in same st as joining, dc in next 7 dc, (2 dc in next dc, dc in next 7 dc) around; join with slip st to first dc: 117 dc.

Rnd 10: Ch 2, 2 dc in same st as joining, dc in next 8 dc, (2 dc in next dc, dc in next 8 dc) around; join with slip st to first dc: 130 dc.

Rnd 11: Ch 2, 2 dc in same st as joining, dc in next 9 dc, (2 dc in next dc, dc in next 9 dc) around; join with slip st to first dc: 143 dc.

Rnd 12: Ch 2, 2 dc in same st as joining, dc in next 10 dc, (2 dc in next dc, dc in next 10 dc) around; join with slip st to first dc: 156 dc.

Rnd 13: Ch 2, 2 dc in same st as joining, dc in next 11 dc, (2 dc in next dc, dc in next 11 dc) around; join with slip st to first dc: 169 dc.

Rnd 14: Ch 2, 2 dc in same st as joining, dc in next 12 dc, (2 dc in next dc, dc in next 12 dc) around; join with slip st to first dc: 182 dc.

Rnd 15: Ch 2, 2 dc in same st as joining, dc in next 13 dc, (2 dc in next dc, dc in next 13 dc) around; join with slip st to first dc: 195 dc.

Rnd 16: Ch 2, 2 dc in same st as joining, dc in next 14 dc, (2 dc in next dc, dc in next 14 dc) around; join with slip st to first dc: 208 dc.

Rnd 17: Ch 2, 2 dc in same st as joining, dc in next 15 dc, (2 dc in next dc, dc in next 15 dc) around; join with slip st to first dc: 221 dc.

Rnds 18 and 19: Ch 2, dc in same st as joining and in each dc around; join with slip st to first dc.

Rnd 20: Ch 2, 2 dc in same st as joining, dc in next 16 dc, (2 dc in next dc, dc in next 16 dc) around; join with slip st to first dc: 234 dc.

Rnd 21: Ch 2, 2 dc in same st as joining, dc in next 17 dc, (2 dc in next dc, dc in next 17 dc) around; join with slip st to first dc: 247 dc.

Rnd 22: Ch 2, 2 dc in same st as joining, dc in next 18 dc, (2 dc in next dc, dc in next 18 dc) around; join with slip st to first dc: 260 dc.

Rnd 23: Ch 2, 2 dc in same st as joining, dc in next 19 dc, (2 dc in next dc, dc in next 19 dc) around; join with slip st to first dc: 273 dc.

Rnd 24: Ch 2, 2 dc in same st as joining, dc in next 20 dc, (2 dc in next dc, dc in next 20 dc) around; join with slip st to first dc: 286 dc.

Rnd 25: Ch 2, 2 dc in same st as joining, dc in next 21 dc, (2 dc in next dc, dc in next 21 dc) around; join with slip st to first dc: 299 dc.

Rnd 26: Ch 2, 2 dc in same st as joining, dc in next 22 dc, (2 dc in next dc, dc in next 22 dc) around; join with slip st to first dc: 312 dc.

Rnd 27: Ch 2, 2 dc in same st as joining, dc in next 23 dc, (2 dc in next dc, dc in next 23 dc) around; join with slip st to first dc: 325 dc.

Rnd 28: Ch 2, 2 dc in same st as joining, dc in next 24 dc, (2 dc in next dc, dc in next 24 dc) around; join with slip st to first dc: 338 dc.

Rnd 29: Ch 2, 2 dc in same st as joining, dc in next 25 dc, (2 dc in next dc, dc in next 25 dc) around; join with slip st to first dc: 351 dc.

Rnds 30 and 31: Ch 2, dc in same st as joining and in each dc around; join with slip st to first dc.

Rnd 32: Ch 2, 2 dc in same st as joining, dc in next 26 dc, (2 dc in next dc, dc in next 26 dc) around; join with slip st to first dc, finish off: 364 dc.

Fairway

With larger size hook and Green, ch 100; with **right** side of Putting Green facing, slip st in any dc.

Row 1: Slip st in next dc on Putting Green, turn; sc in each ch across: 100 sc.

Row 2: Ch 1, turn; sc in each st across, slip st in next 2 dc on Putting Green.

Row 3: Turn; sc in first sc, tr in next sc, (sc in next sc, tr in next sc) across to last 2 sc, sc in last 2 sc.

Rows 4-9: Repeat Rows 2 and 3, 3 times.

Row 10 (Decrease row)**:** Ch 1, turn; sc in each st across to last 4 sts, sc2tog twice, slip st in next 2 dc on Putting Green: 98 sc.

Row 11: Turn; sc in first sc, tr in next sc, (sc in next sc, tr in next sc) across to last 2 sc, sc in last 2 sc.

Rows 12-19: Repeat Rows 2 and 3, 4 times.

Rows 20-51: Repeat Rows 10-19, 3 times; then repeat Rows 10 and 11 once **more**: 90 sts.

Rows 52-69: Repeat Rows 2 and 3, 9 times.

Row 70 (Increase row)**:** Ch 1, turn; sc in each st across to last 2 sts, 2 sc in each of last 2 sts, slip st in next 2 dc on Putting Green: 92 sc.

Row 71: Turn; sc in first sc, tr in next sc, (sc in next sc, tr in next sc) across to last 2 sc, sc in last 2 sc.

Rows 72-79: Repeat Rows 2 and 3, 4 times.

Rows 80-119: Repeat Rows 70-79, 4 times: 100 sts.

Row 120: Ch 1, turn; sc in each st across; finish off.

Border

Row 1: With **wrong** side facing, using larger size hook and working in free loops of beginning ch **(Fig. 3b, page 43)**, join Green with sc in first ch on Fairway **(see Joining With Sc, page 42)**; sc in next ch, (tr in next ch, sc in next ch) across; working in unworked dc on Putting Green, (tr in next dc, sc in next dc) across to last 2 dc, skip next dc, tr in next dc; working in sc on Row 120, sc in first sc, tr in next sc, (sc in next sc, tr in next sc) across to last 2 sc, sc in last 2 sc: 443 sts.

Row 2: Ch 1, turn; sc in each st across.

Row 3: Ch 1, turn; sc in first 2 sc, tr in next sc, (sc in next sc, tr in next sc) across to last 2 sc, sc in last 2 sc.

Row 4: Ch 1, turn; sc in each st across; finish off.

The Rough

Row 1: With **right** side facing, using larger size hook and working in sc on Row 4 of Border, join Dk Green with slip st in first sc; ch 2, hdc in same st as joining and in next sc, dc in next sc and in each sc across to last 2 sc increasing 8 dc evenly spaced along rounded edge of Putting Green, hdc in last 2 sc: 451 sts.

Row 2: Ch 2, turn; hdc in first 2 hdc, slip st in Back Loop Only of next dc **(Fig. 1, page 43)**, (ch 7, slip st in Back Loop Only of next dc) across to last 2 hdc, hdc in **both** loops of last 2 hdc.

Row 3 (Increase row)**:** Ch 2, turn; hdc in first 2 hdc, working behind the loops, dc in free loops of each st across on row **below** previous row **(Fig. 3a, page 43)** increasing 7 dc evenly spaced along rounded edge of Putting Green, hdc in **both** loops of last 2 hdc: 458 sts.

Row 4: Ch 2, turn; hdc in first 2 hdc, slip st in Back Loop Only of next dc, (ch 7, slip st in Back Loop Only of next dc) across to last 2 hdc, hdc in **both** loops of last 2 hdc.

Rows 5-14: Repeat Rows 3 and 4, 5 times: 493 sts.

Finish off.

Small Sand Trap

With larger size hook and Off White, ch 31.

Rnd 1 (Right side)**:** (Sc, dc) 3 times in second ch from hook, (sc in next ch, dc in next ch) 14 times, (sc, dc) 3 times in last ch; working in free loops of beginning ch, (sc in next ch, dc in next ch) 14 times; join with slip st to first sc: 68 sts.

Rnd 2: Ch 1, (sc, dc) in same st as joining and in each of next 5 sts, (sc in next sc, dc in next dc) 14 times, (sc, dc) in each of next 6 sts, (sc in next sc, dc in next dc) 14 times; join with slip st to first sc: 80 sts.

Rnd 3: Ch 1, sc in same st as joining, † (dc, sc) in next dc, dc in next sc, (sc, dc) in next dc, sc in next sc †; repeat from † to † 2 times **more**, (dc in next dc, sc in next sc) 14 times, repeat from † to † 3 times, dc in next dc, (sc in next sc, dc in next dc) 13 times; join with slip st to first sc: 92 sts.

Rnd 4: Ch 1, (sc, dc) in same st as joining, † [sc in next st, dc in next st, (sc, dc) in next st] 5 times, (sc in next sc, dc in next dc) 15 times †, (sc, dc) in next sc, repeat from † to † once; join with slip st to first sc: 104 sts.

Rnd 5: Ch 1, sc in same st as joining, dc in next dc, (sc in next sc, dc in next dc) around; join with slip st to first sc.

Rnd 6: Ch 1, sc in same st as joining, (dc, sc) in each of next 22 sts, (dc in next dc, sc in next sc) 5 times, (dc2tog, sc2tog) 3 times, (dc in next dc, sc in next sc) 4 times, (dc, sc) in each of next 22 sts, dc in next dc, (sc in next sc, dc in next dc) 14 times; join with slip st to first sc, finish off: 142 sts.

Rnd 7: With **right** side facing and using larger size hook, join Dk Green with slip st in same st as joining; ch 2, hdc in same st and in each st around; join with slip st to first hdc.

Rnd 8: Slip st in Front Loop Only of same st as joining **(Fig. 1, page 43)**, ch 7, (slip st in Front Loop Only of next hdc, ch 7) around; join with slip st to **both** loops of first slip st.

Rnd 9: Working behind the loops and in free loops of sts on Rnd 7, (sc, hdc) in first hdc, skip next hdc, ★ (sc, hdc) in next hdc, skip next hdc; repeat from ★ around; join with slip st to **both** loops of first sc, finish off leaving a long end for sewing.

Large Sand Trap

Work same as Small Sand Trap through Rnd 6; do **not** finish off: 142 sts.

Rnds 7 and 8: Ch 1, sc in same st as joining, dc in next dc, (sc in next sc, dc in next dc) around; join with slip st to first sc.

Finish off.

Rnd 9: With **right** side facing and using larger size hook, join Dk Green with slip st in same st as joining; ch 2, hdc in same st and in each st around; join with slip st to first hdc.

Rnd 10: Slip st in Front Loop Only of same st as joining, ch 7, (slip st in Front Loop Only of next hdc, ch 7) around; join with slip st to **both** loops of first slip st.

Rnd 11: Working behind the loops and in free loops of sts on Rnd 9, (sc, hdc) in first hdc, skip next hdc, ★ (sc, hdc) in next hdc, skip next hdc; repeat from ★ around; join with slip st to **both** loops of first sc, finish off leaving a long end for sewing.

GAME PIECES

Flag

With smaller size hook and Yellow, ch 12.

Row 1: Dc in third ch from hook and in next 4 chs, sc in last 5 chs: 10 sts.

Row 2 (Right side)**:** Ch 2, turn; working in Back Loops Only, dc in first 5 sc, sc in last 5 dc.

Note: Mark Row 2 as **right** side.

Row 3: Ch 2, turn; working in Front Loops Only and beginning in first sc, dc2tog, dc in next 3 sc, sc in next 3 dc, sc2tog: 8 sts.

Row 4: Ch 2, turn; working in Back Loops Only and beginning in first sc, dc2tog, dc in next 2 sc, sc in next 2 dc, sc2tog: 6 sts.

Row 5: Ch 2, turn; working in Front Loops Only and beginning in first sc, dc2tog, dc in next sc, sc in next dc, sc2tog: 4 sts.

Row 6: Ch 2, turn; working in Back Loops Only and beginning in first sc, dc2tog, sc2tog: 2 sts.

Row 7: Ch 2, turn; working in Front Loops Only and beginning in first sc, dc2tog: one dc.

Trim: Ch 1, turn; sc evenly across end of rows; working in free loops of beginning ch, 3 sc in ch at base of first dc, sc in each ch across to last ch, 3 sc in last ch; sc evenly across end of rows; slip st in first dc on Row 7, finish off leaving a long end for sewing.

Flag Pole

With smaller size hook and Light Weight White, ch 51; hdc in back ridge of second ch from hook **(Fig. 2, page 43)** and each ch across; finish off leaving a long end for sewing.

Golf Club

With smaller size hook and Grey, ch 10.

Row 1: Sc in back ridge of second ch from hook and each ch across: 9 sc.

Row 2 (Right side)**:** Ch 1, turn; sc in each sc across.

Note: Mark Row 2 as **right** side.

Row 3: Ch 1, turn; sc in first 2 sc, leave remaining 7 sc unworked.

Rows 4-15: Ch 1, turn; sc in first 2 sc; at end of Row 15, finish off leaving a long end for sewing.

Row 16: With **right** side facing and using smaller size hook, join Blue with sc in first sc; sc in last sc: 2 sc.

Rows 17-24: Ch 1, turn; sc in first 2 sc; at end of Row 24, finish off leaving a long end for sewing.

Golf Ball

Rnd 1 (Right side)**:** With smaller size hook and Light Weight White, ch 2, 8 sc in second ch from hook; join with slip st to first sc, finish off leaving a long end for sewing.

FINISHING

Using photo, page 10, as a guide for placement, pin pieces to **right** side of Afghan. Sew in place using matching yarn and long ends.

With Grey, work backstitch between Rnds 1 and 2 of Putting Green **(Fig. 7, page 46)**.

POKER TABLE

AFGHAN NO. 3

POKER TABLE

EASY + **Finished Size:** 36″ x 72″ (91.5 cm x 183 cm)

SHOPPING LIST

Yarn

FOR TABLE

MEDIUM 4 (Medium Weight)
[7 ounces, 426 yards
(197 grams, 389 meters) per skein**]**:

- ☐ Green - 4 skeins
- ☐ Black - 3 skeins

FOR GAME PIECES

LIGHT 3 (Light Weight)
[1.75 ounces, 136 yards
(50 grams, 125 meters) per skein**]**:

- ☐ Off White - 2 skeins
- ☐ Black - 35 yards (32 meters)
- ☐ Blue - 35 yards (32 meters)
- ☐ Yellow - 35 yards (32 meters)
- ☐ Red - 35 yards (32 meters)
- ☐ Green - 35 yards (32 meters)
- ☐ White - 6 yards (5.5 meters)

LACE 0 (Lace Weight)
[350 yards (320 meters) per ball**]**:

- ☐ Off White - 1 ball
- ☐ Navy - 1 ball

[300 yards (274 meters) per ball**]**:

- ☐ Blue Variegated - 1 ball

Crochet Hooks

FOR TABLE

- ☐ Size I (5.5 mm) **or** size needed for gauge

FOR GAME PIECES

- ☐ Size F (3.75 mm)

Additional Supplies

- ☐ Markers (split ring or scrap yarn)
- ☐ Red embroidery floss - 1 hank
- ☐ Black embroidery floss - 1 hank
- ☐ Pins (for Finishing)
- ☐ Yarn needle
- ☐ Tapestry needle

GAUGE INFORMATION

In Table pattern, 13 dc and 8 rows/rnds = 4″ (10 cm)
Gauge Swatch: 4″ (10 cm) square
With largest size hook and Green, ch 15.
Row 1: Dc in fourth ch from hook **(3 skipped chs count as first dc)** and in each ch across: 13 dc.
Rows 2-8: Ch 3 **(counts as first dc)**, turn; dc in next dc and in each dc across.
Finish off.

TABLE

With larger size hook and Green, ch 100; place marker in fifth ch from hook for st placement.

Rnd 1 (Wrong side)**:** 6 Dc in fourth ch from hook **(3 skipped chs count as first dc)**, dc in next ch and in each ch across to last ch, 7 dc in last ch; working in free loops of beginning ch **(Fig. 3b, page 43)**, dc in each ch across ending in marked ch, remove marker; join with slip st to first dc: 204 dc.

Note: Loop a short piece of yarn around the **back** of any stitch on Rnd 1 to mark **right** side.

Rnd 2: Ch 3 **(counts as first dc, now and throughout)**, dc in same st as joining, 2 dc in each of next 6 dc, dc in next 95 dc, 2 dc in each of next 7 dc, dc in last 95 dc; join with slip st to first dc: 218 dc.

Rnd 3: Ch 3, 2 dc in next dc, (dc in next dc, 2 dc in next dc) 6 times, dc in next 96 dc, 2 dc in next dc, (dc in next dc, 2 dc in next dc) 6 times, dc in last 95 dc; join with slip st to first dc: 232 dc.

Rnd 4: Ch 3, 2 dc in next dc, (dc in next 2 dc, 2 dc in next dc) 6 times, dc in next dc, place marker around dc just made for st placement, dc in next 96 dc, place marker around last dc made for st placement, 2 dc in next dc, (dc in next 2 dc, 2 dc in next dc) 6 times, dc in next dc, place marker around dc just made for st placement, dc in each dc across; join with slip st to first dc: 246 dc.

On the following 23 rounds, continue to increase by working 2 dc in one dc.

Rnds 5-27: Ch 3, dc in each dc across to next marker increasing 7 times evenly spaced, dc in marked dc, remove marker and place around dc just made for st placement, dc in each dc across to next marker, dc in marked dc, remove marker and place around dc just made for st placement, dc in each dc across to next marker increasing 7 times evenly spaced, dc in marked dc, remove marker and place around dc just made for st placement, dc in each dc across; join with slip st to first dc: 568 dc.

Rnd 28 (Right side)**:** Ch 3, **turn**; dc in next dc and in each dc around moving markers in same manner; join with slip st to first dc.

Rnd 29: Ch 3, turn; dc in next dc and in each dc around moving markers in same manner; join with slip st to first dc; finish off.

Border

Rnd 1: With **right** side facing and using larger size hook, join Black with sc in same st as joining **(see Joining With Sc, page 42)**; dc in same st, skip next dc, ★ (sc, dc) in next dc, skip next dc; repeat from ★ around moving markers in same manner; join with slip st to first sc: 568 sts.

On the following 11 rounds, **one** increase is made by not skipping a dc and working (sc, dc) in **each** of the next 2 sts (an increase of 2 sts). Continue moving markers in same manner through Rnd 11.

Rnds 2-12: Ch 1, (sc, dc) in same st as joining, skip next dc, ★ [(sc, dc) in next sc, skip next dc] across to next marker, [(sc, dc) in next sc, skip next dc] across to next marker increasing 3 times evenly spaced; repeat from ★ once **more**; join with slip st to first sc: 700 sts.

Finish off.

GAME PIECES

Back of Poker Card (Make 19)

With smaller size hook and holding 3 strands of thread together throughout (one of **each** color), ch 12.

Row 1 (Right side)**:** (Sc, dc) in second ch from hook, skip next ch, ★ (sc, dc) in next ch, skip next ch; repeat from ★ 3 times **more**, sc in last ch: 11 sts.

Note: Loop a short piece of yarn around any stitch to mark Row 1 as **right** side.

Rows 2-12: Ch 1, turn; (sc, dc) in first sc, skip next dc, ★ (sc, dc) in next sc, skip next dc; repeat from ★ 3 times **more**, sc in last sc.

Finish off.

Trim: With **right** side facing, using smaller size hook and working in sts across Row 12, join Light Weight Off White with sc in first sc; sc evenly around entire piece working 3 sc in each corner; join with slip st to first sc, finish off leaving a long end for sewing.

Front of Poker Card (Make 3)

With smaller size hook and Light Weight Off White, ch 12.

Rows 1-12: Work same as Back; at end of Row 12, do **not** finish off: 11 sts.

Trim: Ch 1, turn; sc evenly around entire piece working 3 sc in each corner; join with slip st to first sc, finish off leaving a long end for sewing.

APPLIQUÉS

Heart: With smaller size hook and Red embroidery floss, ch 4; in fourth ch from hook work (3 dc, 3 hdc, ch 1, dc, ch 1, 3 hdc, 3 dc, ch 3, slip st); finish off leaving a long end for sewing.

Spade: With smaller size hook and Black embroidery floss, ch 4; in fourth ch from hook work (3 dc, 3 hdc, ch 1, dc, ch 1, 3 hdc, 3 dc, ch 3, slip st), ch 3 for stem, slip st in second ch from hook and in next ch, slip st in same ch of beginning ch; finish off leaving a long end for sewing.

Diamond - Row 1: With smaller size hook and Red embroidery floss, ch 3, 2 hdc in third ch from hook **(2 skipped chs count as first hdc)**: 3 hdc.

Row 2: Ch 2 **(counts as first hdc, now and throughout)**, turn; hdc in first 2 hdc, 2 hdc in last hdc: 5 hdc.

Row 3: Ch 2, turn; hdc in first 4 hdc, 2 hdc in last hdc: 7 hdc.

Rows 4 and 5: Ch 1, turn; YO, insert hook in first st, YO and pull up a loop, YO, insert hook in next st, YO and pull up a loop, YO and draw through all 5 loops on hook, hdc in each hdc across to last 2 sts, (YO, insert hook in **next** st, YO and pull up a loop) twice, YO and draw through all 5 loops on hook: 3 sts.

Row 6: Ch 1, turn; YO, insert hook in first st, YO and pull up a loop, (YO, insert hook in **next** st, YO and pull up a loop) twice, YO and draw through all 7 loops on hook; finish off leaving a long end for sewing: one st.

Sew one Appliqué to each of the Front of Poker Cards.

Poker Chips (Make 50 total)

Make 10 Chips **each** in the following colors: Yellow, Blue, Black, Green and Red.

Rnd 1 (Right side)**:** With smaller size hook, ch 2; 10 sc in second ch from hook; join with slip st to first sc.

Note: Mark Rnd 1 as **right** side.

Rnd 2: Ch 1, 2 sc in same st as joining and in each sc around; join with slip st to first sc: 20 sc.

To change colors in sc, work until there are 2 loops on hook, drop yarn, with new yarn, YO and draw through both loops on hook **(Fig. A)**. Work over color not being used **(Fig. B)**, holding it with normal tension.

Fig. A

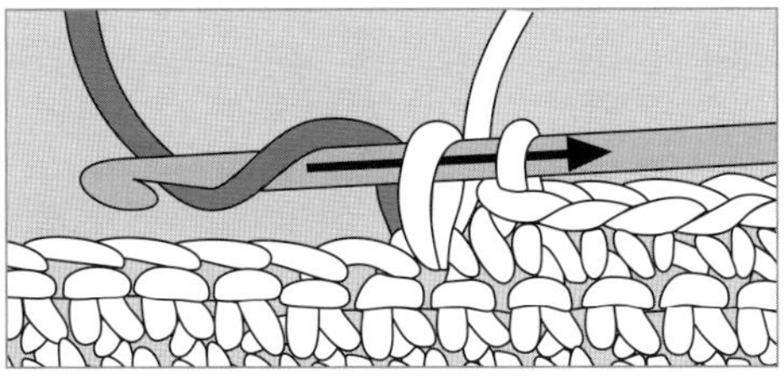

Fig. B

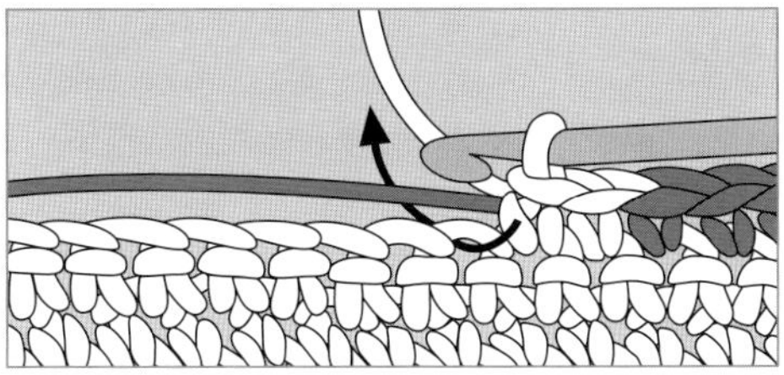

Rnd 3: Ch 1, 2 sc in same st as joining, sc in next sc changing to Light Weight Off White, 2 sc in next sc, sc in next sc changing to color, ★ 2 sc in next sc, sc in next sc changing to Off White, 2 sc in next sc, sc in next sc changing to color; repeat from ★ around; join with slip st to first sc, finish off leaving a long end of color for sewing (cut Off White).

Dealer Chip

Rnd 1 (Right side)**:** With smallest size hook and White, ch 2; 10 sc in second ch from hook; join with slip st to first sc.

Note: Mark Rnd 1 as **right** side.

Rnd 2: Ch 1, 2 sc in same st as joining and in each sc around; join with slip st to first sc: 20 sc.

Rnd 3: Ch 1, 2 sc in same st as joining, sc in next sc, (2 sc in next sc, sc in next sc) around; join with slip st to first sc: 30 sc.

Rnd 4: Ch 1, 2 sc in same st as joining, sc in next 2 sc, (2 sc in next sc, sc in next 2 sc) around; join with slip st to first sc, finish off leaving a long end for sewing: 40 sc.

With Black embroidery floss and using straight stitch **(Fig. 8, page 46)**, add a "D" to Chip.

FINISHING

Using photo, page 18, as a guide for placement, pin pieces to **right** side of Afghan. Sew in place using matching yarn and long ends.

POOL TABLE

AFGHAN NO. 4

POOL TABLE

EASY + **Finished Size:** 48″ x 66″ (122 cm x 167.5 cm)

SHOPPING LIST

Yarn (Medium Weight)

[7 ounces, 426 yards
(197 grams, 389 meters) per skein**]**:

- ☐ Tan - 5 skeins
- ☐ Brown - 2 skeins
- ☐ Black - 1 skein
- ☐ Black Fleck - 50 yards (45.5 meters)
- ☐ Off White - 32 yards (29.5 meters)
- ☐ Lt Brown - 30 yards (27.5 meters)
- ☐ White - 22 yards (20 meters)
- ☐ Yellow - 9 yards (8 meters)
- ☐ Orange - 9 yards (8 meters)
- ☐ Red - 9 yards (8 meters)
- ☐ Purple - 9 yards (8 meters)
- ☐ Burgundy - 9 yards (8 meters)
- ☐ Blue - 9 yards (8 meters)
- ☐ Green - 9 yards (8 meters)

Crochet Hooks

FOR POOL TABLE

- ☐ Size I (5.5 mm)
  or size needed for gauge

FOR GAME PIECES

- ☐ Size H (5 mm)

Additional Supplies

- ☐ Pins (for Finishing)
- ☐ Yarn needle
- ☐ Tapestry needle
- ☐ Lt Blue embroidery floss

GAUGE INFORMATION

In Felt pattern, 12 dc and 9 rows = 4″ (10 cm)
Gauge Swatch:
5¼″w x 4″h (13.25 cm x 10 cm)
With larger size hook and Tan, ch 18.
Work same as Felt for 9 rows: 16 dc.
Finish off.

STITCH GUIDE

SINGLE CROCHET 2 TOGETHER (abbreviated sc2tog)
Pull up a loop in each of next 2 sts, YO and draw through all 3 loops on hook **(counts as one sc)**.

DOUBLE CROCHET 2 TOGETHER (abbreviated dc2tog) (uses next 2 sc)
★ YO, insert hook in **next** sc, YO and pull up a loop, YO and draw through 2 loops on hook; repeat from ★ once **more**, YO and draw through all 3 loops on hook **(counts as one dc)**.

POOL TABLE

Felt

Felt is worked across length of Table.

With larger size hook and Tan, ch 168; place marker in third ch from hook for Edging placement.

Row 1 (Right side)**:** Working in back ridge of chs **(Fig. 2, page 43)**, 2 dc in fourth ch from hook **(3 skipped chs count as first dc)**, (skip next ch, 2 dc in next ch) across to last 2 chs, skip next ch, dc in last ch: 166 dc.

Note: Loop a short piece of yarn around any stitch to mark Row 1 as **right** side.

Row 2: Ch 3 **(counts as first dc, now and throughout)**, turn; 2 dc in sp **before** next dc **(Fig. 5, page 44)**, (skip next 2 dc, 2 dc in sp **before** next dc) across to last 3 dc, skip next 2 dc, dc in last dc.

Rows 3-86: Ch 3, turn; 2 dc in sp **before** next dc, (skip next 2 dc, 2 dc in sp **before** next dc) across to last 3 dc, skip next 2 dc, dc in last dc.

Edging: Ch 3, turn; 2 dc in first dc, dc in next 82 dc, place marker in last dc made for Side Pocket placement, dc in same st and in next 82 dc, 3 dc in last dc; working in end of rows, 2 dc in first row, dc in next row, (2 dc in next row, dc in next row) across; working in free loops of beginning ch **(Fig. 3b, page 43)**, 3 dc in first ch, dc in next 82 chs, place marker in last dc made for Side Pocket placement, dc in same st and in next 82 chs, 3 dc in marked ch, remove marker; working in end of rows, 2 dc in first row, dc in next row, (2 dc in next row, dc in next row) across; join with slip st to first dc, finish off: 600 dc.

Pockets

CORNER

Row 1: With **right** side facing and using larger size hook, join Black with dc in first dc of any corner 3-dc group **(see Joining With Dc, page 42)**; 2 dc in same st, 3 dc in each of next 2 dc, skip next dc, slip st in next dc: 9 dc.

Row 2: Ch 1, turn; sc in first dc and in each dc across, skip next dc on Edging, slip st in next dc.

Row 3: Ch 3, turn; 2 dc in first sc and in each sc across, skip next dc on Edging, slip st in next dc: 19 dc.

Rows 4-6: Repeat Rows 2 and 3 once, then repeat Row 2 once **more**: 39 sc.

Row 7: Ch 3, turn; 2 dc in first sc, (dc in next sc, 2 dc in next sc) across, skip next dc on Edging, slip st in next dc: 60 dc.

Row 8: Ch 1, turn; sc in first dc and in each dc across, skip next dc on Edging, slip st in next dc; finish off.

Repeat on remaining 3 corners.

SIDE

Row 1: With **right** side facing and using larger size hook, join Black with dc in marked dc on long edge, remove marker; 2 dc in same st, 3 dc in each of next 2 dc, skip next dc, slip st in next dc: 9 dc.

Row 2: Ch 1, turn; sc in first dc and in each dc across, skip next dc on Edging, slip st in next dc.

Row 3: Ch 3, turn; 2 dc in first sc and in each sc across, skip next dc on Edging, slip st in next dc: 19 dc.

Rows 4-6: Repeat Rows 2 and 3 once, then repeat Row 2 once **more**: 39 sc.

Row 7: Ch 3, turn; dc in first sc and in each sc across, skip next dc on Edging, slip st in next dc.

Row 8: Ch 1, turn; sc in first dc and in each dc across, skip next dc on Edging, slip st in next dc; finish off.

Repeat on remaining long edge.

Sections

Each long edge will have one Section beginning with **right** side facing, with the remaining Section beginning with **wrong** side facing.

CORNER TO SIDE POCKET

Row 1: Working across long edge and using larger size hook, join Brown with dc in same st on Edging as Corner Pocket slip st; dc in next 65 dc, skip first sc on Side Pocket, slip st in next sc: 66 dc.

Row 2: Ch 1, turn; sc in first dc and in each dc across, slip st in first 3 sc on Corner Pocket.

Row 3: Ch 1, turn; beginning in first sc, dc2tog, dc in each sc across to last 2 sc, dc2tog, skip next sc on Side Pocket, slip st in next sc: 64 dc.

Row 4: Ch 1, turn; sc in first dc and in each dc across, slip st in next 3 sc on Corner Pocket.

Row 5 (Increase row)**:** Ch 1, turn; 2 dc in first sc, dc in each sc across to last sc, 2 dc in last sc, skip next sc on Side Pocket, slip st in next sc: 66 dc.

Row 6 (Increase row)**:** Ch 1, turn; 2 sc in first dc, sc in each dc across to last dc, 2 sc in last dc, slip st in next 3 sc on Corner Pocket: 68 sc.

Rows 7-13: Repeat Rows 5 and 6, 3 times; then repeat Row 5 once **more**; at end of Row 13, finish off: 82 dc.

Repeat across remaining 3 sections of long edge.

CORNER TO CORNER POCKET

Row 1: With **right** side of short edge facing and using larger size hook, join Brown with dc in first unworked dc on Edging **after** Corner Pocket; dc in each dc across, skip first sc on next Corner Pocket, slip st in next sc: 113 dc.

Row 2: Ch 1, turn; sc in first dc and in each dc across, slip st in first 3 sc on next Corner Pocket.

Row 3: Ch 1, turn; beginning in first sc, dc2tog, dc in each sc across to last 2 sc, dc2tog, skip next sc on next Corner Pocket, slip st in next sc: 111 dc.

Row 4: Ch 1, turn; sc in first dc and in each dc across, slip st in next 3 sc on next Corner Pocket.

Row 5 (Increase row)**:** Ch 1, turn; 2 dc in first sc, dc in each sc across to last sc, 2 dc in last sc, skip next sc on next Corner Pocket, slip st in next sc: 113 dc.

Row 6 (Increase row)**:** Ch 1, turn; 2 sc in first dc, sc in each dc across to last dc, 2 sc in last dc, slip st in next 3 sc on next Corner Pocket: 115 sc.

Rows 7-13: Repeat Rows 5 and 6, 3 times; then repeat Row 5 once **more**; at end of Row 13, finish off: 129 dc.

Repeat across remaining short edge but do **not** finish off at end of Row 13.

Border

Rnd 1 (Right side)**:** Do **not** turn; (slip st, ch 1, sc) in next sc, ★ sc in each unworked sc across Pocket, beginning in same st on Pocket as slip st, sc2tog, sc in each dc across to last dc before next Pocket, sc2tog ending in same st on Pocket as slip st; repeat from ★ around; join with slip st to first sc.

Rnd 2: Ch 3, **turn**; dc in next sc and in each sc around; join with slip st to first dc.

Rnd 3: Ch 3, do **not** turn; dc in next dc and in each dc around increasing 5 dc evenly spaced across each Corner Pocket; join with slip st to first dc, finish off.

GAME PIECES

Solid Pool Balls

Make one **each** in the following colors: White, Yellow, Orange, Red, Purple, Burgundy, Blue, Green, and Black.

Rnd 1 (Right side)**:** With smaller size hook, ch 4, 11 dc in fourth ch from hook; join with slip st to top of beginning ch: 12 sts.

Note: Mark Rnd 1 as **right** side.

Rnd 2: Ch 3, dc in same st as joining, 2 dc in next dc and in each dc around; join with slip st to first dc, finish off leaving a long end for sewing.

Striped Pool Balls

Make one **each** using the following colors for Rnd 2: Yellow, Orange, Red, Purple, Burgundy, Blue, and Green.

Rnd 1 (Right side)**:** With White and using smaller size hook, ch 4, 11 dc in fourth ch from hook; join with slip st to top of beginning ch, finish off: 12 sts.

Note: Mark Rnd 1 as **right** side.

Rnd 2: With **right** side facing and using smaller size hook, join next color with dc in same st as joining; dc in same st, 2 dc in next dc and in each dc around; join with slip st to first dc, finish off leaving a long end for sewing.

Rack

With Lt Brown and using smaller size hook, ch 183; being careful **not** to twist ch, join with slip st to form a ring.

Rnd 1 (Right side)**:** Ch 3, 4 dc in same ch as joining, dc in next 60 chs, (5 dc in next ch, dc in next 60 chs) twice; join with slip st to first dc, finish off leaving a very long end for sewing.

Pool Stick (Make 2)

With Black Fleck and using smaller size hook, ch 6.

Row 1: Sc in second ch from hook and in each ch across: 5 sc.

Rows 2-52: Ch 1, turn; sc in each sc across.

Row 53: Ch 1, turn; sc in first sc, sc2tog, sc in last 2 sc: 4 sc.

Rows 54-62: Ch 1, turn; sc in each sc across.

Row 63: Ch 1, turn; sc in first sc, sc2tog, sc in last sc: 3 sc.

Rows 64-72: Ch 1, turn; sc in each sc across; at end of Row 72, finish off.

Note: Mark Row 72 as **right** side.

Row 73: With **wrong** side facing and using smaller size hook, join Off White with sc in first sc **(see Joining With Sc, page 42)**; sc in next 2 sc: 3 sc.

Rows 74-110: Ch 1, turn; sc in each sc across.

Row 111: Ch 1, turn; sc in first sc, sc2tog: 2 sc.

Rows 112-161: Ch 1, turn; sc in first 2 sc; at end of Row 161, finish off.

Row 162: With **right** side facing and using smaller size hook, join White with sc in first sc; sc in last sc: 2 sc.

Rows 163-165: Ch 1, turn; sc in first 2 sc; at end of Row 165, finish off.

FINISHING

Using photo as a guide for placement, pin pieces to **right** side of Afghan. Sew in place using matching yarn and long ends.

Using satin stitch **(Fig. 9, page 46)** and Lt Blue embroidery floss, sew a few stitches to tip of Pool Sticks for chalk.

SLOT MACHINE

AFGHAN NO. 5

SLOT MACHINE

EASY +

Finished Size: 45″ x 80½″ (114.5 cm x 204.5 cm)

SHOPPING LIST

Yarn

MEDIUM 4 (Medium Weight)
[4 ounces, 203 yards
(113 grams, 186 meters) per skein]:

- ☐ Red - 7 skeins
- ☐ Black - 6 skeins
- ☐ Lt Grey - 2 skeins

[4 ounces, 208 yards
(113 grams, 190 meters) per skein]:

- ☐ Red Sparkle - 3 skeins

LIGHT 3 (Light Weight)
[1.75 ounces, 161 yards
(50 grams, 147 meters) per skein]:

- ☐ White - 2 skeins
- ☐ Black - 1 skein

Crochet Hook

- ☐ Size I (5.5 mm)
  or size needed for gauge

Additional Supplies

- ☐ Silver metallic embroidery floss - 4 hanks
- ☐ Pins (for Finishing)
- ☐ Yarn needle

GAUGE INFORMATION

With Light Weight Yarn,
in Reel pattern, 15 sts = 4″ (10 cm);
10 rows = 3″ (7.5 cm)
With Medium Weight Yarn,
16 dc = 5″(12.75 cm);
9 rows = 4″ (10 cm)

Gauge Swatch #1: 4″w x 3″h (10 cm x 7.5 cm)
With White, ch 16.
Work same as Reel for 10 rows: 15 sts.
Finish off.

Gauge Swatch #2: 5″w x 4″h
(12.75 cm x 10 cm)
With Red, ch 18.

Row 1: Dc in fourth ch from hook **(3 skipped chs count as first dc)** and in each ch across: 16 dc.

Rows 2-9: Ch 3 **(counts as first dc)**, turn; dc in next dc and in each dc across.
Finish off.

STITCH GUIDE

TREBLE CROCHET (abbreviated tr)
YO twice, insert hook in st indicated, YO and pull up a loop (4 loops on hook), (YO and draw through 2 loops on hook) 3 times.

SINGLE CROCHET 2 TOGETHER (abbreviated sc2tog)
Pull up a loop in each of next 2 sts, YO and draw through all 3 loops on hook **(counts as one sc)**.

HALF DOUBLE CROCHET 2 TOGETHER (abbreviated hdc2tog) (uses next 2 chs)
★ YO, insert hook in **next** ch, YO and pull up a loop; repeat from ★ once **more**, YO and draw through all 5 loops on hook **(counts as one hdc)**.

DOUBLE CROCHET 2 TOGETHER (abbreviated dc2tog) (uses next 2 sts)
★ YO, insert hook in **next** st, YO and pull up a loop, YO and draw through 2 loops on hook; repeat from ★ once **more**, YO and draw through all 3 loops on hook **(counts as one dc)**.

SLOT MACHINE

Reel (Make 3)

With White, ch 40.

Row 1 (Right side)**:** Sc in second ch from hook, (dc in next ch, sc in next ch) across: 39 sts.

Note: Loop a short piece of yarn around any stitch to mark Row 1 as **right** side.

Row 2: Ch 2 **(does not count as a st)**, turn; dc in first sc, (sc in next dc, dc in next sc) across.

Row 3: Ch 1, turn; sc in first dc, (dc in next sc, sc in next dc) across.

Rows 4-25: Repeat Rows 2 and 3, 11 times.

Finish off.

Trim: With **right** side facing, join Lt Grey with slip st in first sc on Row 25; ch 2 **(does not count as a st)**, 2 dc in same st, dc in each st across to last sc, 3 dc in last sc; work 25 dc evenly spaced across end of rows; working in free loops of beginning ch **(Fig. 3b, page 43)**, 3 dc in first ch, dc in next 37 chs, 3 dc in next ch; work 25 dc evenly spaced across ends of rows, dc in same st as joining slip st; skip beginning ch-2 and join with slip st to first dc, finish off leaving a long end for sewing: 136 dc.

ASSEMBLY

Thread yarn needle with long end.
With **wrong** sides of long edges together and working through **both** loops on **both** pieces, whipstitch 2 Reels together **(Fig. 6a, page 45)**, beginning in center dc of first 3-dc group and ending in center dc of next 3-dc group.
Whipstitch remaining Reel in same manner.

Number 7 (Make 3)

TOP

With Red, ch 11.

Row 1 (Right side)**:** Sc in second ch from hook and in each ch across: 10 sc.

Note: Mark Row 1 as **right** side.

Row 2: Ch 1, turn; sc in each sc across.

Row 3: Turn; slip st in first 2 sc, sc in next 6 sc, leave last 2 sc unworked: 6 sc.

Row 4: Ch 1, turn; 2 sc in first sc, sc in next 3 sc, sc2tog.

Row 5: Ch 1, turn; beginning in first sc, sc2tog, sc in next 3 sc, 2 sc in last sc.

Row 6: Ch 1, turn; 2 sc in first sc, sc in next 3 sc, sc2tog.

Rows 7 and 8: Ch 1, turn; sc in each sc across.

Row 9: Ch 1, turn; 2 sc in first sc, sc in next 4 sc, 2 sc in last sc: 8 sc.

Row 10: Ch 1, turn; beginning in first sc, sc2tog, sc in next 5 sc, 2 sc in last sc.

Row 11: Ch 1, turn; sc in each sc across.

Row 12: Ch 1, turn; beginning in first sc, sc2tog, sc in next 5 sc, 2 sc in last sc.

Row 13: Ch 1, turn; sc in first 6 sc, sc2tog: 7 sc.

Row 14: Ch 1, turn; sc in each sc across.

Row 15: Ch 1, turn; sc in first 6 sc, 2 sc in last sc: 8 sc.

Rows 16-20: Ch 1, turn; sc in each sc across.

Place marker around last sc made on Row 20 for Bottom placement.

Row 21: Turn; slip st in first 3 sc, sc in next 4 sc, 2 sc in last sc: 6 sc.

Row 22: Ch 1, turn; 2 sc in first sc, sc in next 3 sc, leave last 2 sc unworked: 5 sc.

Row 23: Turn; slip st in first 3 sc, sc in next sc, 2 sc in last sc; finish off: 3 sc.

BOTTOM

Row 1: With **wrong** side facing and working in end of rows, join Red with sc in marked row **(see Joining With Sc, page 42)**; remove marker, sc in next 4 rows, 2 sc in next row: 7 sc.

Row 2: Ch 1, turn; 2 sc in first sc, sc in next 4 sc, sc2tog.

Row 3: Ch 1, turn; beginning in first sc, sc2tog, sc in next 4 sc, 2 sc in last sc.

Row 4: Ch 1, turn; 2 sc in first sc, sc in next 4 sc, sc2tog.

Row 5: Ch 1, turn; sc in first 6 sc, 2 sc in last sc: 8 sc.

Rows 6 and 7: Ch 1, turn; sc in each sc across.

Row 8: Ch 1, turn; 2 sc in first sc, sc in next 5 sc, sc2tog.

Rows 9-20: Ch 1, turn; sc in each sc across.

Finish off.

Trim: With **wrong** side facing, join Light Weight Black with sc in first sc on Row 20 of Bottom; 2 sc in same st, sc in next 6 sc, 3 sc in last sc; sc in end of next 30 rows and in next slip st on Row 3 of Top, 3 sc in last slip st; sc in end of next 2 rows; working in free loops of beginning ch, 3 sc in ch at base of first sc, sc in next 8 chs, 3 sc in last ch; sc in end of next 2 rows; 3 sc in first sc on Row 2, sc in next sc and in end of next 20 rows; 3 sc in first sc on Row 23, sc in next sc, 3 sc in last sc, skip last 3 slip sts, 2 sc in next sc on Row 21, sc in next sc and in next 3 slip sts, sc in end of last 20 rows; join with slip st to first sc, finish off leaving a long for sewing.

Using long end, sew one Number 7 to each Reel, being sure they are centered and lined up across.

Reels Edging

Rnd 1: With **right** side facing and working across top edge, join Lt Grey with slip st in center dc of first 3-dc group; ch 2 **(does not count as a st)**, 3 dc in same st, † dc in next 27 dc, (dc2tog working in joining dc of 2 Reels, dc in next 27 dc) twice, 3 dc in next 3-dc group, dc in next 39 dc †, 3 dc in next 3-dc group, repeat from † to † once; join with slip st to first dc, finish off: 256 dc.

Rnd 2: With **right** side facing and working across top edge, join Medium Weight Black with slip st in center dc of first 3-dc group; ch 3 **(counts as first dc, now and throughout)**, (dc, ch 2, 2 dc) in same st, ★ dc in next dc and in each dc across to center dc of next 3-dc group, (2 dc, ch 2, 2 dc) in center dc; repeat from ★ 2 times **more**, dc in next dc and in each dc across; join with slip st to first dc: 268 dc and 4 ch-2 sps.

Rnd 3: Ch 3, turn; ★ dc in next dc and in each dc across to next ch-2 sp, (2 dc, ch 2, 2 dc) in ch-2 sp; repeat from ★ 3 times **more**, dc in last dc; join with slip st to first dc: 284 dc and 4 ch-2 sps.

Rnds 4-9: Ch 3, turn; ★ dc in next dc and in each dc across to next ch-2 sp, (2 dc, ch 2, 2 dc) in ch-2 sp; repeat from ★ 3 times **more**, dc in next dc and in each dc across; join with slip st to first dc: 380 dc and 4 ch-2 sps.

Finish off.

Top

Row 1: With **right** side facing, join Red with slip st in first ch-2 sp; ch 3, dc in next dc and in each dc across to next ch-2 sp, dc in ch-2 sp: 119 dc.

Rows 2-40: Ch 3, turn; dc in next dc and in each dc across.

Finish off.

Bottom

With **wrong** side facing, work same as Top along opposite long edge; do **not** finish off.

Border

Rnd 1: Ch 3, do **not** turn; 2 dc in same st, † dc in next dc and in each dc across to last dc, 3 dc in last dc; 2 dc in end of next 40 rows, dc in next ch-2 sp on Reels Edging, dc in next dc and in each dc across to next ch-2 sp, dc in ch-2 sp, 2 dc in end of next 40 rows †, 3 dc in first dc on Row 40, repeat from † to † once; join with slip st to first dc: 716 dc.

Rnds 2 and 3: Ch 3, turn; dc in next dc and in each dc around working 3 dc in center dc of each 3-dc group; join with slip st to first dc.

Finish off.

Rnd 4: With **right** side facing, join Lt Grey with slip st in center dc of first 3-dc group; dc in next dc and in each dc around working 3 dc in center dc of each 3-dc group; join with slip st to first dc.

Rnd 5: Ch 3, turn; dc in next dc and in each dc around working 3 dc in center dc of each 3-dc group; join with slip st to first dc, finish off.

Rnd 6: With **right** side facing, join Medium Weight Black with slip st in center dc of first 3-dc group; dc in next dc and in each dc around working 3 dc in center dc of each 3-dc group; join with slip st to first dc.

Rnds 7-12: Ch 3, turn; dc in next dc and in each dc around working 3 dc in center dc of each 3-dc group; join with slip st to first dc.

Finish off.

Small Star (Make 6)

With Red Sparkle, ch 4; join with slip st to form a ring.

Rnd 1 (Right side)**:** Ch 3, 9 dc in ring; join with slip st to first dc: 10 dc.

Note: Mark Rnd 1 as **right** side.

Rnd 2: ★ † Ch 5, sc in second ch from hook, hdc in next ch, dc in next ch, tr in last ch, skip next dc on Rnd 1 †, slip st in next dc; repeat from ★ 3 times **more**, then repeat from † to † once; join with slip st in st at base of beginning ch-5, finish off: 5 points.

Rnd 3: With **right** side facing, join Light Weight Black with sc in ch at tip of any point; sc in same st and in next 4 sts, sc in free loop of next 4 chs, ★ 2 sc in ch at tip of next point, sc in next 4 sts, sc in free loop of next 4 chs; repeat from ★ around; join with slip st to first sc, finish off leaving a long end for sewing.

Large Star (Make 21)

Holding two strands of Red Sparkle together, work same as Small Star.

Coin Tray

With Medium Weight Black, ch 87.

Row 1 (Right side)**:** Dc in fourth ch from hook **(3 skipped chs count as first dc)** and in each ch across: 85 dc.

Note: Mark Row 1 as **right** side.

Rows 2-10: Ch 3, turn; dc in next dc and in each dc across.

Finish off.

Trim: With **right** side facing, join Lt Grey with slip st in second dc on Row 10; dc in next dc and in each dc across to last dc, skip last dc; † working in end of rows, 3 dc in first row, 2 dc in next 8 rows, 3 dc in last row †; working in free loops of beginning ch, skip first ch, dc in next ch and in each ch across to last ch, skip last ch; repeat from † to † once; join with slip st to first dc, finish off leaving a long end for sewing.

Coin (Make 10)

Rnd 1 (Right side)**:** Holding one strand **each** of Lt Grey and Silver embroidery floss together, ch 2, 8 hdc in second ch from hook; join with slip st to first hdc.

Note: Mark Rnd 1 as **right** side.

Rnd 2: Ch 1, turn; 2 hdc in same st as joining and in each hdc around; join with slip st to first hdc, finish off leaving a long end for sewing.

Coin Slot

With Lt Grey, ch 20.

Row 1 (Right side)**:** Hdc in second ch from hook and in each ch across: 19 hdc.

Note: Mark Row 1 as **right** side.

Row 2: Ch 2 **(does not count as a st)**, turn; hdc in each hdc across.

Row 3: Ch 1, turn; sc in first 6 hdc, slip st in next 7 hdc, sc in last 6 hdc.

Row 4: Ch 1, turn; sc in first 6 sc, ch 7, skip next 7 slip sts, sc in last 6 sc: 12 sc and 7 chs.

Row 5: Ch 1, turn; sc in each sc and in each ch across: 19 sc.

Rows 6 and 7: Ch 2 **(does not count as a st)**, turn; hdc in each st across.

Finish off.

Handle Stick

With Lt Grey, ch 70.

Row 1 (Right side)**:** Hdc in second ch from hook and in each ch across to last 7 chs, hdc2tog, hdc in last 5 chs; finish off leaving a long for sewing.

Note: Mark Row 1 as **right** side.

Handle Ball

Rnd 1 (Right side)**:** With Red Sparkle, ch 2, 8 hdc in second ch from hook; do **not** join, place marker to indicate the beginning of the rnd **(see Markers, page 42)**.

Note: Mark Rnd 1 as **right** side.

Rnd 2: 2 Hdc in each hdc around: 16 hdc.

Rnd 3: (2 Hdc in next hdc, hdc in next hdc) around: 24 hdc.

Rnd 4: (2 Hdc in next hdc, hdc in next 2 hdc) around; slip st in next hdc, finish off leaving a long end for sewing.

Finishing

Using photo, page 32, as a guide for placement, pin pieces to **right** side of Afghan. Sew in place using matching yarn and long ends.

GENERAL INSTRUCTIONS

ABBREVIATIONS

ch(s)	chain(s)
cm	centimeters
dc	double crochet(s)
dc2tog	double crochet 2 together
hdc	half double crochet(s)
hdc2tog	half double crochet 2 together
mm	millimeters
Rnd(s)	Round(s)
sc	single crochet(s)
sc2tog	single crochet 2 together
sp(s)	space(s)
st(s)	stitch(es)
tr	treble crochet(s)
YO	yarn over

SYMBOLS & TERMS

★ — work instructions following ★ as many **more** times as indicated in addition to the first time.

† to † — work all instructions from first † to second † **as many** times as specified.

( ) or [ ] — work enclosed instructions **as many** times as specified by the number immediately following **or** work all enclosed instructions in the stitch or space indicated **or** contains explanatory remarks.

colon (:) — the number(s) given after a colon at the end of a row or round denote(s) the number of stitches or spaces you should have on that row or round.

CROCHET TERMINOLOGY		
UNITED STATES		INTERNATIONAL
slip stitch (slip st)	=	single crochet (sc)
single crochet (sc)	=	double crochet (dc)
half double crochet (hdc)	=	half treble crochet (htr)
double crochet (dc)	=	treble crochet (tr)
treble crochet (tr)	=	double treble crochet (dtr)
double treble crochet (dtr)	=	triple treble crochet (ttr)
triple treble crochet (tr tr)	=	quadruple treble crochet (qtr)
skip	=	miss

CROCHET HOOKS																	
U.S.	B-1	C-2	D-3	E-4	F-5	G-6	7	H-8	I-9	J-10	K-10½	L-11	M/N-13	N/P-15	P/Q	Q	S
Metric - mm	2.25	2.75	3.25	3.5	3.75	4	4.5	5	5.5	6	6.5	8	9	10	15	16	19

BEGINNER	Projects for first-time crocheters using basic stitches. Minimal shaping.
EASY	Projects using yarn with basic stitches, repetitive stitch patterns, simple color changes, and simple shaping and finishing.
INTERMEDIATE	Projects using a variety of techniques, such as basic lace patterns or color patterns, mid-level shaping and finishing.
EXPERIENCED	Projects with intricate stitch patterns, techniques and dimension, such as non-repeating patterns, multi-color techniques, fine threads, small hooks, detailed shaping and refined finishing.

GAUGE

Exact gauge is essential for proper size. Before beginning your Afghan, make the sample swatch given in the individual instructions in the yarn and hook specified. After completing the swatch, measure it, counting your stitches and rows/rounds carefully. If your swatch is larger or smaller than specified, **make another, changing hook size to get the correct gauge**. Keep trying until you find the size hook that will give you the specified gauge.

MARKERS

Markers are used to help distinguish the beginning of each round being worked. Place a 2″ (5 cm) scrap piece of yarn before the first stitch of each round, moving marker after each round is complete.

JOINING WITH SC

When instructed to join with a sc, begin with a slip knot on the hook. Insert hook in stitch or space indicated, YO and pull up a loop, YO and draw through all 3 loops on hook.

JOINING WITH DC

When instructed to join with a dc, begin with a slip knot on the hook. YO, holding loop on hook, insert hook in stitch or space indicated, YO and pull up a loop (3 loops on hook), (YO and draw through 2 loops on hook) twice.

Yarn Weight Symbol & Names	LACE 0	SUPER FINE 1	FINE 2	LIGHT 3	MEDIUM 4	BULKY 5	SUPER BULKY 6	JUMBO 7
Type of Yarns in Category	Fingering, size 10 crochet thread	Sock, Fingering, Baby	Sport, Baby	DK, Light Worsted	Worsted, Afghan, Aran	Chunky, Craft, Rug	Super Bulky, Roving	Jumbo, Roving
Crochet Gauge* Ranges in Single Crochet to 4" (10 cm)	32-42 sts**	21-32 sts	16-20 sts	12-17 sts	11-14 sts	8-11 sts	6-9 sts	5 sts and fewer
Advised Hook Size Range	Steel*** 6 to 8, Regular hook B-1	B-1 to E-4	E-4 to 7	7 to I-9	I-9 to K-10½	K-10½ to M/N-13	M/N-13 to Q	Q and larger

*GUIDELINES ONLY: The chart above reflects the most commonly used gauges and hook sizes for specific yarn categories.

** Lace weight yarns are usually crocheted with larger hooks to create lacy openwork patterns. Accordingly, a gauge range is difficult to determine. Always follow the gauge stated in your pattern.

*** Steel crochet hooks are sized differently from regular hooks–the higher the number, the smaller the hook, which is the reverse of regular hook sizing.

BACK OR FRONT LOOP ONLY

Work only in loop(s) indicated by arrow **(Fig. 1)**.

Fig. 1

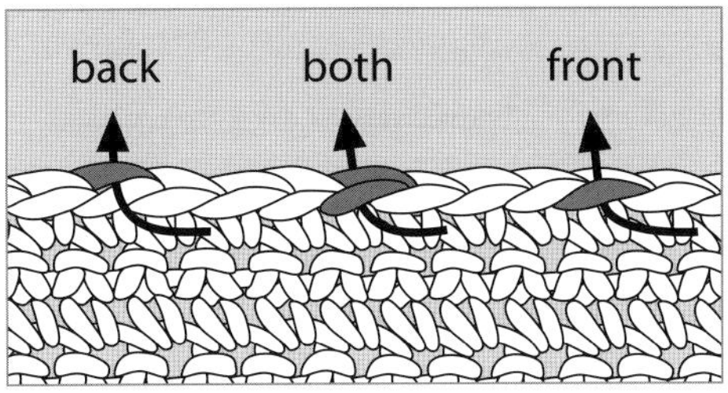

BACK RIDGE

Work only in loops indicated by arrows **(Fig. 2)**.

Fig. 2

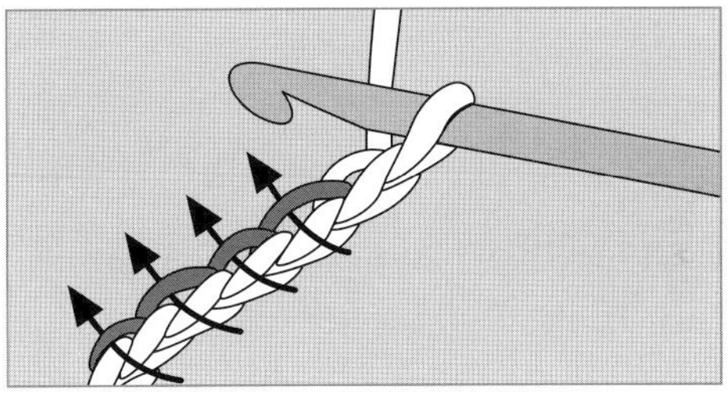

FREE LOOPS

After working in Back or Front Loops Only on a row or round, there will be a ridge of unused loops. These are called the free loops. Later, when instructed to work in the free loops of the same row or round, work in these loops **(Fig. 3a)**.

When instructed to work in free loops of a chain, work in loop indicated by arrow **(Fig. 3b)**.

Fig. 3a

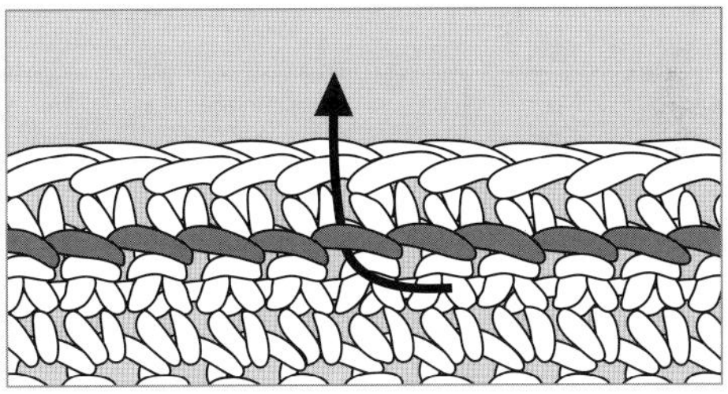

Fig. 3b

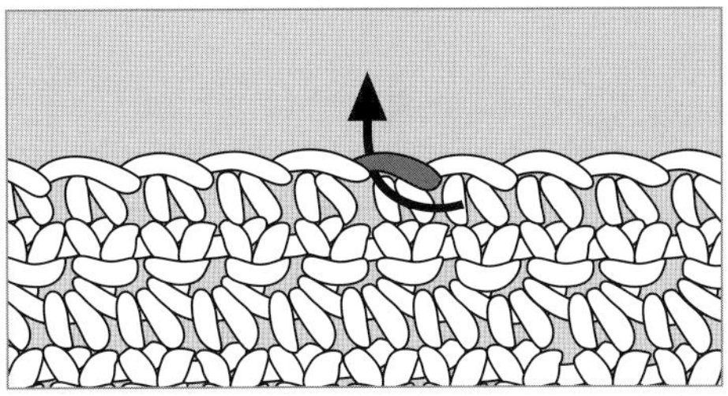

CHANGING COLORS

Work the last stitch to within one step of completion, hook new yarn **(Fig. 4a or 4b)** and draw through all loops on hook.

Fig. 4a

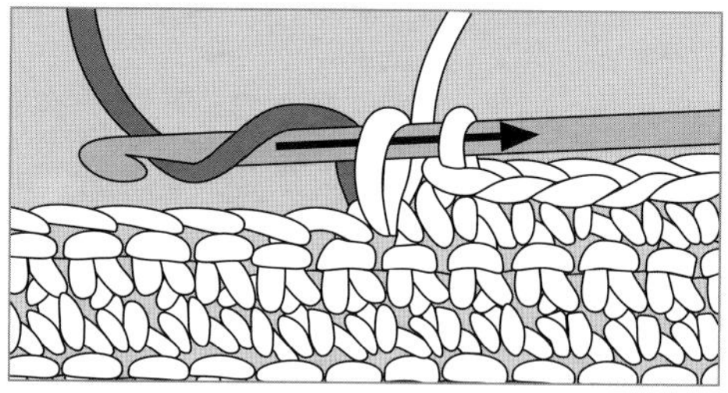

Fig. 4b

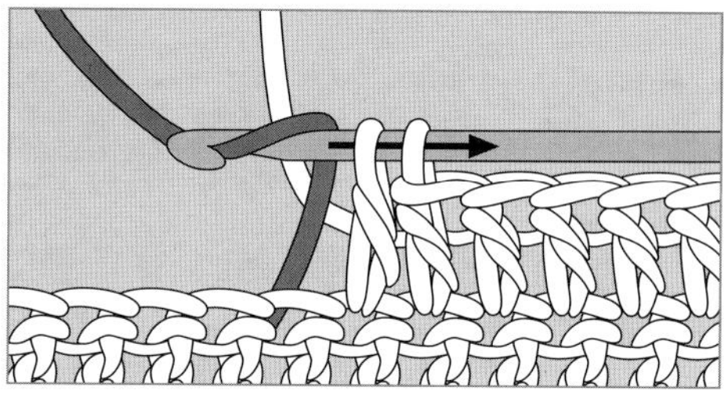

WORKING IN A SPACE BEFORE A STITCH

When instructed to work in a space **before** a stitch or in spaces **between** stitches, insert hook in space indicated by arrow **(Fig. 5)**.

Fig. 5

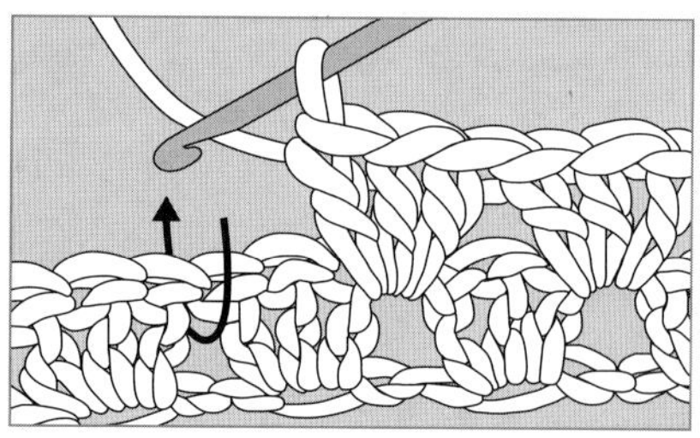

WHIPSTITCH

Place two pieces with **wrong** sides together. Beginning in center of corner, sew through both pieces once to secure the beginning of the seam, leaving an ample yarn end to weave in later. Insert the needle from **front** to **back** through both loops/layer(s) on **both** pieces **(Figs. 6a or b)**. Bring the needle around and insert it from **front** to **back** through next loops/layer(s) on **both** pieces. Continue in this manner across ending in next corner and keeping the sewing yarn fairly loose.

Fig. 6a

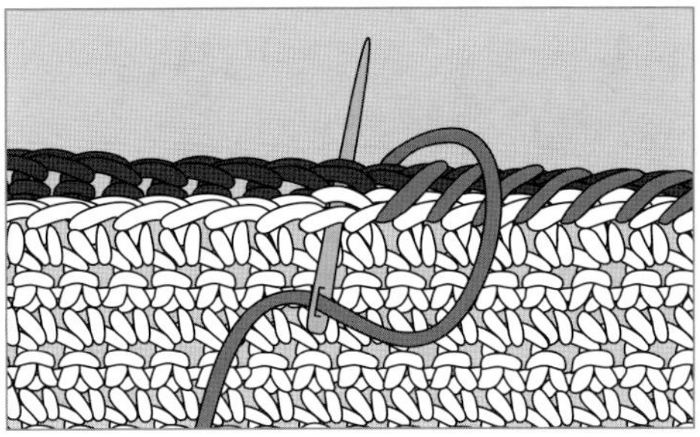

Fig. 6b

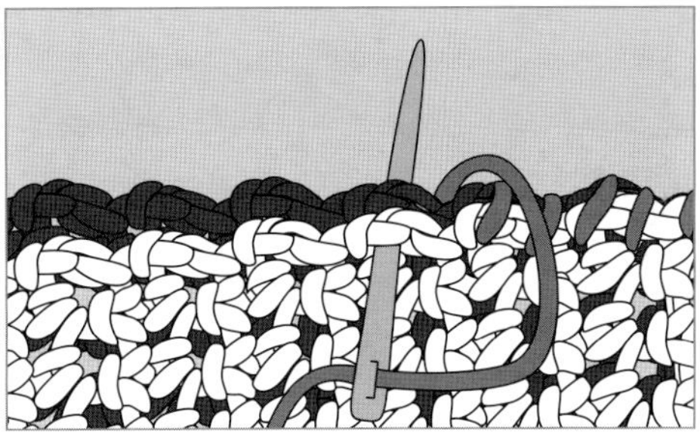

EMBROIDERY STITCHES

Backstitch

Backstitch is worked from **right** to **left**. Come up at 1, go down at 2 and come up at 3 **(Fig. 7)**. The second stitch is made by going down at 1 and coming up at 4.

Fig. 7

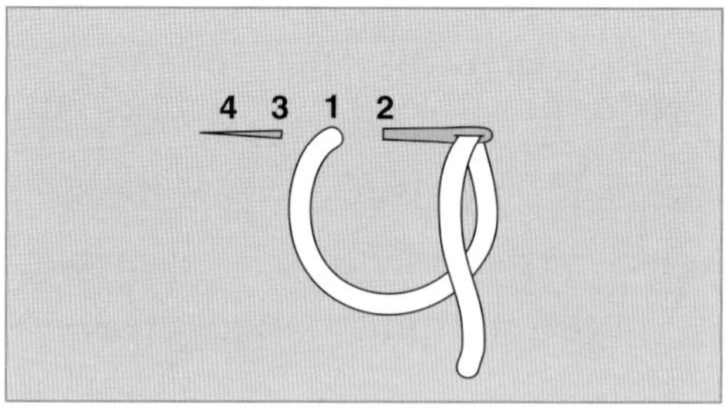

Straight Stitch

Straight stitch is just what the name implies, a single, straight stitch. Come up at 1 and go down at 2 **(Fig. 8)**.

Fig. 8

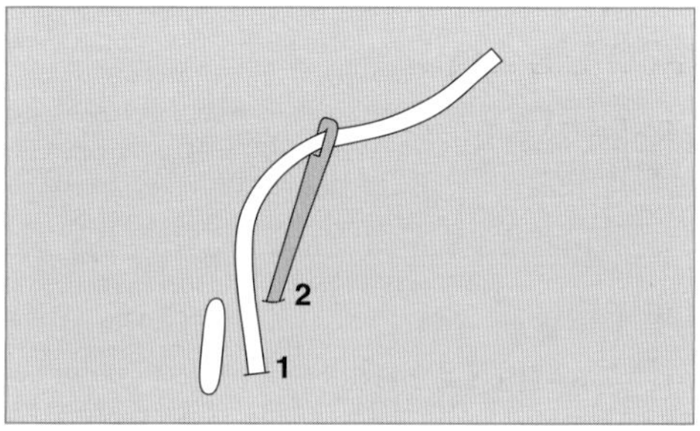

Satin Stitch

Satin stitch is a series of straight stitches worked side-by-side so they touch but do not overlap **(Fig. 9)**. Come up at odd numbers and go down at even numbers.

Fig. 9

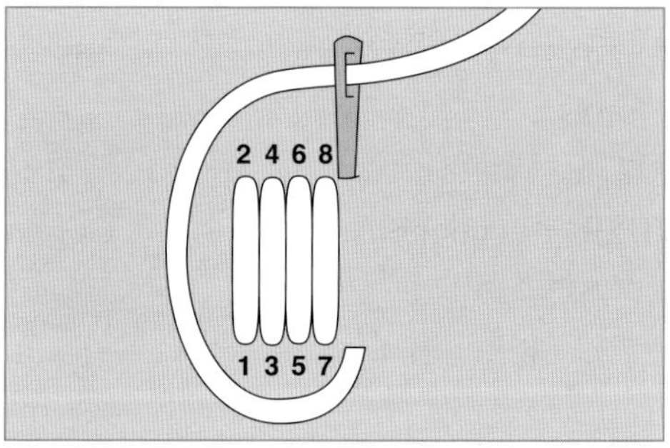

YARN INFORMATION

The Afghans in this book were made using various weights of yarn. Any brand of the specified weight of yarn may be used. It is best to refer to the yardage/meters when determining how many balls or skeins to purchase. Remember, to arrive at the finished size, it is the GAUGE/TENSION that is important, not the brand of yarn.

For your convenience, listed below are the specific yarn styles and colors used to create our photography models. Because yarn manufacturers make frequent changes in their product lines, you may sometimes find it necessary to use a substitute yarn or to search for the discontinued product at alternate suppliers (locally or online).

BOWLING ALLEY

Lion Brand® Vanna's Choice®

Black - #153 Black

White - #100 White

Red - #113 Scarlet

Lion Brand® Heartland®

Gold - #130 Bryce Canyon

Blue - #109 Olympic

GOLF GREEN

Lion Brand® Vanna's Choice®

Green - #171 Fern

Dk Green - #172 Kelly Green

Olive Green - #173 Dusty Green

White - #100 White

Caron® One Pound™

Off White - #10514 Off White

Patons® Astra™

White - #02751 White

Yellow - #02941 School Bus Yellow

Grey - #02729 Silver Grey Mix

Blue - #02733 Electric Blue

POKER TABLE

Bernat® Super Value™

Green - #00609 Kelly

Black - #07421 Black

Patons® Grace™

Off White - #62008 Natural

Black - #60040 Night

Blue - #62134 Blue Bayou

Yellow - #62622 Sunkissed

Red - #60705 Cardinal

Green - #62700 Emerald

White - #62005 Snow

Aunt Lydia's® Classic Crochet™ Size 10

Off White - #210 Antique White

Navy - #486 Navy

Variegated - #14 Shaded Blues

POOL TABLE

Bernat® Super Value™

Tan - #07469 Honey

Brown - #07483 Walnut

Black - #07421 Black

Bernat® Satin™

Black Fleck - #84040 Black Tweed

Patons® Classic Wool Worsted™

Off White - #00202 Aran

Lion Brand® Vanna's Choice®

Lt Brown - #130 Honey

Red Heart® Classic™

White - #1 White

Yellow - #230 Yellow

Orange - #245 Orange

Red - #902 Jockey Red

Purple - #588 Amethyst

Burgundy - #917 Cardinal

Blue - #849 Olympic Blue

Green - #686 Paddy Green

SLOT MACHINE

Premier® Yarns Deborah Norville Collection™ Everyday® Solids

Red - #100-07 Really Red

Black - #100-12 Black

Lt Grey - #100-23 Mist

Red Heart® Sparkle Soft™

Red Sparkle - #9921 Really Red

Patons® Astra™

White - #02751 White

Black - #02765 Black

MEET THE DESIGNER: Karen Barnes

Karen Barnes is an avid yarn-lover who has been crocheting since the age of 12, taught by her grandmother and later inspired by pattern stitch encyclopedias.

"I crochet almost daily for my children, coworkers, family, and craft shows," she says. "I love yarn! I can walk into any yarn store and have a huge smile on my face."

The school bus driver and mother of two grown children says afghans are her favorite project. "I am open minded and like a good challenge. My pattern stitch encyclopedias are very helpful."

Karen came up with the idea of sports afghans when her son asked her to make special Christmas gifts for his friends. "I searched the Internet, library, and my patterns looking for something that was manly and unique," she explained. "I found manly colors or geometric shapes, but nothing that said 'man' to me." Not a fan of graph patterns, Karen tried to think of items that could be created in an appliqué form.

"I would like to continue designing guy afghans and maybe a wedding dress for my daughter when the day comes," she says. Karen also enjoys sewing, eBay, and traveling with her husband and her mother.

We have made every effort to ensure that these instructions are accurate and complete.
We cannot, however, be responsible for human error, typographical mistakes, or variations in individual work.

Production Team: Instructional/Technical Writer - Linda A. Daley; Editorial Writer - Susan Frantz Wiles; Senior Graphic Artist - Lora Puls; Graphic Artist - Marcus Boyce, Kellie McAnulty and Kytanna McFarlin; Photo Stylist - Lori Wenger; and Photographer - Jason Masters.